PEOPLE AT
THE CENTER OF

THE SPANISH-AMERICAN WAR

By AUDREY KUPFERBERG

BLACKBIRCH PRESS
An imprint of Thomson Gale, a part of The Thomson Corporation

THOMSON
GALE

Detroit • New York • San Francisco • San Diego • New Haven, Conn.
Waterville, Maine • London • Munich

For more information, contact
Blackbirch Press
27500 Drake Rd.
Farmington Hills, MI 48331-3535
Or you can visit our Internet site at http://www.gale.com

LIBRARY OF CONGRESS CATALOGING-IN-PUBLICATION DATA

Kupferberg, Audrey E.
   The Spanish-American War / by Audrey Kupferberg.
     p. cm. — (People at the center of)
Includes bibliographical references and index.
   ISBN 1-56711-924-7 (alk. paper)
   1. Spanish-American War, 1898—Juvenile literature. I. Title. II. Series.
E715.K87 2004
973.8'9—dc22

2004018668

Printed in the United States of America

◎ CONTENTS

THE SPANISH-AMERICAN WAR

Before 1898, all wars fought by Americans occurred on North American soil. The United States had never become embroiled in conflicts between other countries. All this changed with the Spanish-American War, a small-scale skirmish that greatly enhanced America's position on the international political scene.

During the last decade of the nineteenth century, the islands of Cuba, the Philippines, Puerto Rico, and Guam were colonies of Spain. Cuba is located in the Caribbean Sea, ninety miles off the coast of Florida. The Philippines consists of over seven thousand small islands in the southwest Pacific Ocean, with the largest being Luzon. Puerto Rico is one of a chain of islands in the West Indies, located southeast of Florida. Guam is the largest of the Mariana Islands in the Pacific Ocean.

For several decades before the Spanish-American War, Cuban nationalists had sporadically mounted unsuccessful revolts against Spanish rule. One was known as the Ten Years War (1868–1878). Another was called the Guerra Chiquita, or Little War (1879–1880). By the 1890s, nationalist leaders such as José Martí of Cuba and José Rizal and Emilio Aguinaldo y Famy of the Philippines were spearheading new movements for independence from Spain. While Rizal was a pacifist, Martí and Aguinaldo were devising strategies that resulted in armed revolt against Spanish domination of Cuba and the Philippines. The uprising led by Martí began in 1895, while Aguinaldo's revolt broke out the following year.

Grover Cleveland, the U.S. president, wanted America to remain neutral in these conflicts. However, this stance became increasingly tougher to maintain. U.S. businesses had invested more than $50 million in Cuba's sugar crop. Those investments would be in jeopardy if a war broke out between Spain and Cuba. Even though Cleveland eventually began easing his neutral position, he was not renomi-

Legend

→ American Advances
◂····· Spanish Advances
◉ Battles

Map labels:

UNITED STATES

Norfolk

Atlantic
Ocean

Gulf of Mexico

Tampa

SCHLEY

SHAFTER

Key West

SCHLEY

USS *Maine* blows up
(February 15)

Havana

CUBA

SAMPSON

BAHAMA
ISLANDS

Campaign in Santiago
(June 22–July 16)

DOMINICAN
REPUBLIC

Santiago
de Cuba

U.S. destroys
Spanish fleet
(July 3)

JAMAICA

HAITI

San Juan

Guánica

PUERTO
RICO

MILES

MARTINIQUE

CERVERA

MEXICO

BRITISH
HONDURAS

GUATEMALA

HONDURAS

EL SALVADOR

NICARAGUA

COSTA
RICA

PANAMA

COLOMBIA

Caribbean Sea

CERVERA

Curaçao

VENEZUELA

Trinidad

Pacific
Ocean

nated by the Democratic Party during the 1896 presidential race. William
McKinley became the next U.S. president.

The strategy of Valeriano Weyler, a Spaniard who was appointed governor of
Cuba in 1896, added to the crisis. Weyler attempted to crush the revolt by forcing
civilians from their homes into so-called reconcentration camps so that they could
not aid the rebels. Untold thousands became ill and died in the unsanitary camps,
and Weyler came to be known as "the butcher of Cuba."

Despite Weyler's tactics, the Cuban nationalists were as determined as ever to
win independence. A new Spanish president, Práxedes Mateo Sagasta, took office
in 1897. He assumed a more conciliatory approach, even going so far as to grant

Cuba and Puerto Rico self-ruling governments. Sagasta's offer was spurned by the nationalists. They demanded nothing less than total freedom from Spain.

In the United States, newspaper publisher William Randolph Hearst began stoking the fires of war by printing accounts of Weyler's treatment of the Cubans. In order to boost newspaper circulation, he employed "yellow journalism" (reporting that is exaggerated, biased, or inaccurate, rather than factual and objective) in a campaign calculated to manufacture a war between the United States and Spain. In February 1898, the USS *Maine*, an American battleship anchored in Cuba's Havana harbor, was rocked by a mysterious explosion that killed 266 sailors. Hearst responded by printing anti-Spanish accounts featuring such headlines as "War? Sure!"

Hearst's yellow journalism heavily influenced the U.S. Congress and American public, both of which increasingly were in favor of U.S. intervention. "Remember the *Maine!* To hell with Spain" became the battle cry of those anxious to avenge the slaughter.

William McKinley's policy toward Cuba was aligned with this way of thinking. He was unwavering in his insistence that the United States take an active part in resolving the crisis. Initially, he hoped the United States could maintain neutrality while playing the role of mediator. But when the Spanish disregarded a list of ultimatums issued by McKinley, in which he demanded less antagonistic treatment of the Cubans, a war seemed inevitable. On April 21, 1898, the president ordered U.S. Navy ships to blockade Cuba and prevent Spanish soldiers and supplies from reaching the island. Three days later, the U.S. Congress declared war on Spain.

Not every American embraced the war. A number of notable citizens, including novelist-journalist Mark Twain, spoke out against the fighting. They believed that the purpose of U.S. intervention was imperialistic rather than humanitarian, that the United States was primarily interested in establishing colonies and exerting its influence across the globe.

Meanwhile, U.S. forces were battling the Spanish in the Philippines and Cuba. One week into the fighting, U.S. Navy admiral George Dewey took Manila Bay in the Philippines without suffering a single casualty. This easy victory foreshadowed success on all fronts.

The Cuban theater of war centered on McKinley's blockade. The cordoning off of the island began in Havana and quickly spread. On June 1, the Spanish fleet was trapped in the harbor of Santiago de Cuba, a city located on the island's southern coast. One month later, it endeavored to escape, but was swiftly immobilized. Concurrently, on July 1, U.S. land forces decisively defeated the Spanish in the battle of Santiago de Cuba. Theodore Roosevelt, commander of the Rough Riders, an independent military unit attached to the U.S. Fifth Army Corps, emerged from the fighting a national hero.

The Spanish surrendered Santiago de Cuba to the Americans in mid-July. U.S. troops landed in Puerto Rico on July 25, but all fighting ceased on August 12. In October, delegates from the United States and Spain convened in Paris to negotiate a peace treaty. No representatives were invited from the Spanish colonies whose destinies were being deliberated.

The Spanish-American War officially ended on December 10, when the accord, known as the Treaty of Paris, was signed. Cuba was granted independence, while Puerto Rico, Guam, and the Philippines became U.S. territories. However, Filipino nationalists, headed by Aguinaldo, instigated an armed revolt against the United States, which lasted until 1902.

The fighting in the Spanish-American War lasted just ten weeks. However, the victory gave the United States its first overseas possessions and signaled that the former British colonies had matured into a world power.

GROVER CLEVELAND

Grover Cleveland was born in Caldwell, New Jersey, in 1837. He became a lawyer and was elected mayor of Buffalo, New York, and then governor of New York. As governor, he earned nationwide acclaim for battling corruption in state politics. In 1884, he was elected the twenty-second U.S. president and served one term. He lost his 1888 bid to stay in office, but was reelected in 1892.

The islands of Cuba, Puerto Rico, Guam, and the Philippines at that time were colonies of Spain. Nationalists—particularly in Cuba and the Philippines—increasingly were pressuring Spain for independence. This growing conflict was threatening to escalate into a military confrontation.

Grover Cleveland's cabinet poses for a portrait. As president, Cleveland wanted to avoid U.S. involvement in Cuba's fight for independence.

Cleveland opposed direct American involvement in the struggle. However, anti-Spanish sentiment in the United States was being sparked by newspaper accounts of the Spaniards' cruelty to the Cuban population. U.S. companies also had over $50 million invested in Cuban sugar crops and trade. The increasing tensions were putting these investments at risk.

While Cleveland lobbied for a settlement between the Cuban nationalists and the Spanish, he chose not to respond directly to the escalating crisis. On June 12, 1895, he even signed a proclamation that stated that the United States would maintain its neutrality in any future hostilities between Spain and its colonies. Meanwhile, he was faced with a U.S. Congress that increasingly favored the Cuban nationalists and was growing hostile to Cleveland's stance. The House of Representatives and Senate even passed resolutions favoring Cuban independence. Adding to the president's troubles was a brutal domestic economic depression and a steep increase in unemployment among American wage earners.

As his term in office neared its conclusion, Cleveland partially altered his neutral stance. Wanting to be reelected, he conceded that the United States might have to become involved if Spain and Cuba were unable to resolve their issues.

Cleveland's increasing unpopularity resulted in his losing the 1896 Democratic Party presidential nomination. He retired to Princeton, New Jersey, and died in 1908.

Cleveland faced hostility from Congress over his desire to remain neutral in Cuba's conflict with Spain.

INSPIRED CUBAN RESISTANCE TO SPANISH RULE

José Martí was born José Julian Martí y Pérez in Havana, Cuba's largest city, in 1853. During his childhood, he came to understand that his homeland was divided between the wealthy upper classes, who enjoyed power and affluence by aligning themselves with the Spanish, and the lower classes and intellectuals, who yearned to see Cuba an independent nation. While in his teens, he spent a year in prison for expressing the view that Cuba deserved its own government. Then he went into exile in Spain, where he studied law and philosophy at the University of Saragossa. He spent his early adulthood traveling, writing, and speaking out in favor of Cuban independence.

Martí was a poet, patriot, and leader of the Cuban resistance against Spanish rule. He authored poems and articles on life in Cuba under Spanish control and the adverse conditions existing throughout Latin America. His subjects ranged from life in Cuba's jails and the escalating nationalist movement to his thoughts on justice, camaraderie, and liberty. In 1881, he settled in New York City and began stepping up his campaign for Cuban self-government. Nine years later, he and Rafael Serra, a fellow exile, cofounded La Liga (The League), an activist, nationalist-oriented political group consisting of Cuban exiles. In 1892, he and other Cuban nationalists created El Partido Revolucionario Cubano (Cuban Revolutionary Party) to fight for Cuban independence. Through his writings and revolutionary activities, Martí and others like him kept alive the ongoing conflict between Cuba and Spain that led to the Spanish-American War.

José Martí led Cuban rebels in their fight for independence from Spanish rule.

By late 1894, El Partido Revolucionario had raised sufficient money to purchase the ships and arms needed to mount its revolt against Spain. In January, three boatloads of fighters set off from the Florida coast to Cuba but were seized by U.S. authorities. Martí was not present in Cuba when the fighting against the Spanish began on February 24, 1895.

That April, Martí arrived in Cuba and joined the struggle. He died while fighting the Spanish in Dos Rios, located in Cuba's Oriente Province.

Martí, a political activist and writer, worked in New York City to promote resistance to Spanish rule in Cuba. He joined the revolution in Cuba in April 1895.

JOSÉ RIZAL

José Rizal was born in Calamba, Laguna, the Philippines, in 1861. He attended the University of St. Thomas in Manila and the University of Madrid. He then traveled throughout Europe and studied medicine at the University of Heidelberg.

Rizal was an ardent supporter of Filipino nationalism. In 1886, he authored *Noli me Tangere* (loosely translated as *Touch Me Not*), a novel in which he censured Spain's presence in the Philippines and criticized the Catholic Church for endorsing colonization. He then wrote additional books and articles in which he called for Filipino liberation. Even though Rizal was a pacifist, he predicted that Filipino peasants would take up arms against the Spanish. His writings played a significant role in encouraging his countrymen to resist Spanish rule.

In July 1892, Rizal established the Liga Filipina (Philippine League), an antiviolence, social reform–oriented political group that advocated Filipino independence and national unity. In retaliation, the Spanish authorities immediately banished him to Dapitan, a city on the Philippine island of Mindanao. He remained there for four years, during which time he practiced medicine and conducted scientific experiments.

While Rizal was in exile, many of his nationalist colleagues began advocating violence as a means to achieve independence. The most famous was Emilio Aguinaldo y Famy, who headed a band of nationalists that wished to seize control of the Philippines and establish an independent government. As a pacifist, Rizal criticized Aguinaldo's methods.

In 1896, Rizal requested that he be allowed to enlist in the Spanish army and work as a surgeon in Cuba. While he was planning a trip to Spain to sign up, Filipino nationalists began their revolt. Rizal had not yet left the Philippines when he was arrested, tried, unjustly convicted of treason, and executed by a firing squad.

Through his writings, Filipino nationalist José Rizal urged his countrymen to resist Spanish rule.

EMPLOYED HARSH TACTICS TO QUELL CUBAN NATIONALISTS

Valeriano Weyler y Nicolau was born in Palma, Spain, in 1838. He attended military school in Toledo and began a career in the Spanish army. He served his country in various locations, including Cuba, the Dominican Republic, the Philippines, and the Canary Islands. He rose to the rank of general and earned a reputation as a strict disciplinarian.

By 1896, Cuban nationalists were mounting a rebellion against Spanish rule. The Spanish government sent Weyler to the island. His mission was to quell the uprising and bring about political stability. He was appointed governor of Cuba and given complete authority over its people.

Weyler was frustrated by the tactics of the rebels, who were blending into the civilian population and randomly attacking the Spanish troops. He came to believe that the Spaniards could distinguish between Cuban fighters and nonfighters only if the two groups were separated. Additionally, he wished to prevent the civilians from aiding the nationalists who were hiding out and regrouping in rural areas. For these reasons, he devised a "reconstruction plan" in which he ordered the displacement of hundreds of thousands of Cuban men, women, and children from their rural communities to "reconcentration camps." The camps were ill equipped with food and medical supplies. In them, countless thousands of Cubans died of hunger and assorted illnesses. For his treatment of the Cuban civilians, Weyler earned the nickname "the butcher of Cuba."

Weyler's policies only succeeded in further angering the Cuban nationalists and inciting them to step up their fight against Spain. Newspaper reports about the camps also outraged the American public and intensified their

This illustration shows the miserable conditions of Valeriano Weyler's reconcentration camps, where thousands of Cubans died.

General Weyler treated civilians so brutally that he was called "the butcher of Cuba."

compassion for the plight of the Cuban people. Weyler's situation worsened when a portion of his troops needed to be dispatched to the Pacific to quash the rebellion that was mounting among Filipino nationalists. The governor found himself weakened militarily. He resigned his post at the end of 1897 and returned to Spain.

Weyler was later appointed Spain's minister of war on three separate occasions. He died in 1930.

16 THE SPANISH-AMERICAN WAR

WILLIAM MCKINLEY

William McKinley was born in Niles, Ohio, in 1843. He fought with the Twenty-third Ohio Volunteers in the Civil War (1861–1865), practiced law, and was elected to the U.S. House of Representatives and the Ohio governorship. In 1896, he became the twenty-fifth U.S. president.

Unlike his predecessor, Grover Cleveland, McKinley was determined to become involved in the affairs of other nations—and in the conflict between Spain and its colonies. By doing so, he hoped to protect and expand U.S. business investments. If Spain remained in control of Cuba, America's investments in the island would remain under the thumb of a strong European power. With Spain out of the picture, the United States could increase its control over Cuba's profitable sugar crop. Also, McKinley wished that Cuba be granted independence on humanitarian grounds and pledged that the United States would recognize a free Cuba.

At first, McKinley hoped that the United States would remain neutral as he intervened in the crisis. However, in early February 1898, a letter written two months earlier by Enrique Dupuy de Lóme, Spain's ambassador to the United States, was made public. In the letter, de Lóme harshly criticized McKinley's policies. Then on February 15, 1898, 266 sailors died in the aftermath of an explosion on board the USS *Maine*, an American battleship. At the time, the *Maine* was anchored in Havana harbor on an authorized visit to Cuba.

McKinley still wished to avoid the further shedding of American blood on foreign soil and presented Spain with a list of ultimatums in an effort to secure more humane treatment of the Cubans. The Spanish did not respond, however, and war seemed imminent. On March 9, the U.S. Congress authorized the spending of $50 million to fortify the American military. Three weeks later, a U.S. Navy court of inquiry determined that the *Maine* explosion was no accident; the ship was destroyed by a mine. (In subsequent decades, historians have disputed this finding. The true cause of the explosion remains undetermined.)

President William McKinley involved America in the conflict with Spain to protect American investments in Cuba.

Spain's refusal to negotiate and the USS Maine explosion led Congress to authorize war. Here McKinley signs the Declaration of War.

On April 21, McKinley directed that the navy begin a blockade of Cuba. Finally, on April 24, the U.S. Congress declared war on Spain. In his role as commander in chief, McKinley directed the U.S. military effort in the Spanish defeat. McKinley won reelection in 1900 but was assassinated the following year.

Práxedes Mateo Sagasta was born in Torrecilla de Cameros, Spain, in 1825. He became involved in politics while studying engineering in Madrid, and on two occasions was forced into exile for opposing the rule of Spain's Queen Isabella II. In 1869, he took part in the revolution that caused her downfall. In 1870, Sagasta began his off and on service as Spain's prime minister.

Sagasta once more assumed the role of prime minister in October 1897, two months after an anarchist murdered his predecessor, Antonio Cánovas y Castillo. In this capacity, he was his country's primary policy maker and political strategist before and during the Spanish-American War.

As prime minister, Castillo had promised—and failed—to contain the Cuban nationalists who were rebelling against Spanish rule. Sagasta assumed a more moderate, conciliatory stance. In an effort to avoid U.S. intervention in Cuba, he agreed to allow Cuba and Puerto Rico self-ruling governments. The Cuban nationalists refused to accept his offering; their goal was complete independence. Before the issue could be resolved, the U.S. Congress declared war against Spain.

The Spanish viewed the United States as an opportunistic country that wished to strip Spain of its colonies. They believed that the Americans would never be able to overpower the noble Spanish military that was steeped in tradition. However, the Spanish suffered a quick and humiliating defeat. At the war's conclusion, the country was forced to surrender control of Cuba and Puerto Rico. In the wake of the Spanish defeat, Sagasta's political rivals condemned his policies as treachery against Spain.

Sagasta left office in 1899 but served as Spain's prime minister one final time, from 1901 to 1902. He died in 1903.

Práxedes Mateo Sagasta, hoping to prevent U.S. interference in Spain's colonies, granted self-rule to Cuba and Puerto Rico.

William Randolph Hearst was born in San Francisco in 1863. At age twenty-three, he took control of the *San Francisco Examiner*, which his wealthy father had accepted as compensation for a gambling debt. In 1895, he purchased the *New York Morning Journal* and started an evening edition the following year. Hearst quickly established a reputation not only for hiring top-notch writers and artists but also for printing articles that featured eye grabbing, exaggerated headlines.

William Randolph Hearst caused anti-Spanish feeling to grow in America by printing newspaper headlines like these.

Hearst's prewar "yellow journalism" helped influence American opinion in favor of the Cubans in their revolt against Spanish rule. To create controversy in order to increase newspaper sales—the *Journal* was immersed in a circulation war with the rival *New York World*—Hearst printed a constant barrage of articles and editorial cartoons depicting the Spanish as brutes and butchers. In early February 1898, he published a letter, written the previous December by Enrique Dupuy de Lóme, Spain's ambassador to the United States, which was disapproving of William McKinley's policies and actions. The letter had come into the possession of Cuban nationals in New York, who made it public. Hearst printed it under the headline, "The Worst Insult to the United States in Its History."

In the resulting uproar, McKinley insisted on an apology from the Spanish authorities, and de Lóme was ordered to resign his post and return to Spain. The scandal soon was overshadowed by the sinking of the USS *Maine*. Hearst continued pounding his war drum by running articles with headlines like "War? Sure!" Once war was declared, he even traveled to Cuba to supervise his reporters who were covering the fighting.

Hearst served in the U.S. House of Representatives for four years (1903–1907). During the 1920s, he constructed an extraordinary castle on his ranch in San Simeon, California. All the while, he managed his media empire, which eventually consisted of several dozen newspapers, magazines, radio stations, and motion picture companies. He died in 1951.

Hearst often stretched the truth in his articles about the Spaniards' treatment of Cubans.

MARK TWAIN

Mark Twain is the pen name of Samuel Langhorne Clemens. He was born in Florida, Missouri, in 1835. He spent his early life as a printer's apprentice, Mississippi riverboat pilot, and journalist. He authored his first best seller, *The Innocents Abroad*, in 1869 and subsequently wrote such classic American novels as *The Adventures of Tom Sawyer*, *The Prince and the Pauper*, *The Adventures of Huckleberry Finn*, *A Connecticut Yankee in King Arthur's Court*, and *The Tragedy of Pudd'nhead Wilson*.

LIBERTY TRACTS. No. 1.

THE

CHICAGO LIBERTY MEETING

HELD AT

CENTRAL MUSIC HALL

APRIL 30. 1899

Mark Twain joined the Anti-Imperialist League to protest U.S. foreign policy. A league tract is shown above.

Twain already was a celebrated writer when the Spanish-American War began. The conflict was a popular cause among the majority of Americans and Twain first supported the fighting, which he felt might lead to freedom for Cuba and the Philippines. He quickly altered his opinion and became a vehement critic of war when he came to believe that the United States went into battle for the purpose of imperialism—to establish colonies and wield power across the world.

Twain observed that an uneasy peace was preferable to war. He wrote of the irony of a U.S. foreign policy that presented itself as being well-meaning and compassionate but that saw war and its accompanying strife as the only solution to dealing with international crises.

During the war, Twain became active in the Anti-Imperialist League, which was formed on June 15, 1898, to protest the expected U.S. annexation of the Philippines and additional expansionist American foreign policies. Other prominent members included labor leader Samuel Gompers, industrialist-philanthropist Andrew Carnegie, and psychologist-philosopher William James. Carnegie even proposed to purchase the Philippines from Spain for $20 million and grant the colony its independence. After the signing of the Treaty of Paris, interest in the league declined and it ultimately ceased to exist.

Twain's last years were burdened by a series of failed business ventures and the deaths of his beloved wife, Olivia Langdon Clemens, and three of their four children. He died in 1910.

Twain opposed America's war with Spain, believing the United States only wanted to gain new territories.

GEORGE DEWEY

DEFEATED THE SPANISH FLEET IN THE PHILIPPINES

George Dewey was born in Montpelier, Vermont, in 1837. He graduated from the U.S. Naval Academy at Annapolis, fought for the Union in the Civil War, and held various posts at sea and on land through the 1890s.

By 1897, Dewey had risen to the rank of commodore. He was appointed commander of the U.S. Navy's Asiatic squadron, which put him in charge of American naval forces in the Pacific. A firm and aggressive commander, he insisted on being well supplied with armaments in case the United States went to war with Spain.

On May 1, 1898, just over one week after the U.S. Congress declared war, Dewey led his forces in an assault on the Philippines. His ships entered Manila Bay and passed through mined waters while firing at the mainland. As they did so, not a single mine exploded. The fleet of Spanish ships defending the bay was severely outdated and undermanned. Although the Spanish sailors fought bravely, they were doomed from the start. Without suffering a single casualty, Dewey defeated them and took control of the bay. During the battle, 8 Americans were wounded; Spanish losses added up to 167 killed and 214 wounded.

Dewey then advanced into and took the Spanish naval base at Cavite and the city of Manila. His quick victory so early in the fighting indicated that the United States would emerge triumphant in the Spanish-American War. For the time being, however, he had no army to deploy in a land assault of the Philippines. For assistance, he turned to the Filipino nationalist Emilio Aguinaldo y Famy.

Aguinaldo and Dewey soon clashed over the issue of Filipino self-rule. While Aguinaldo hoped that the war would lead to independence for his country, Dewey and the Americans had no intention of liberating the Philippines. Just before the U.S. Senate was set to vote on the treaty that would end the war and make the Philippines a U.S. possession, armed conflict broke out between Aguinaldo's forces and the Americans. These hostilities lasted five years, through 1902.

For his heroics, Dewey was promoted to admiral of the navy. He emerged from the war a national hero and became president of the general board of the navy. He died in 1917.

George Dewey led American naval forces at Manila Bay in the Philippines, quickly scoring victory over the Spanish fleet.

Dewey's U.S. fleet destroys Spanish warships in Manila Bay. Spain's ships were outdated and undermanned.

Admiral William T. Sampson commanded the U.S. blockade of Cuba, which cut off the Spanish from supplies and reinforcements.

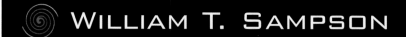

WILLIAM T. SAMPSON

William Thomas Sampson was born in Palmyra, New York, in 1840. He graduated from the U.S. Naval Academy at Annapolis, fought for the Union in the Civil War, and served in the navy at various posts at sea and on land. He also taught science and headed the physics department at Annapolis and eventually became the academy's superintendent.

In 1897, Sampson, by then an admiral in the U.S. Navy, was named commander of the battleship USS *Iowa*. He headed a board of inquiry that examined events surrounding the USS *Maine* explosion. Just before the U.S. Congress declared war on Spain, he was named commander of all American military troops in the North Atlantic.

Primarily, Sampson planned and directed the U.S. blockading effort of Cuba, a strategy that proved essential to quickly winning the war. Initially, he believed that a direct attack of Havana would be the most efficient military strategy. However, his superiors in Washington ordered him not to imperil the

Admiral Sampson's flagship, USS Iowa *(above), fired the first shot in the Battle of Santiago Bay.*

U.S. fleet by taking such a bold step. Instead, his fleet of twenty-six ships set up a blockade of Havana. The blockade rapidly expanded across the northern and then the southern Cuban coasts and prevented the Spanish from shipping men and supplies to and from the island.

On June 1, Sampson and Winfield Scott Schley, commander of the navy's fleet of ships called the "flying squadron," cornered the remaining Spanish fleet in the harbor of Santiago de Cuba on the southern end of the island. At the beginning of July, the fleet attempted to elude the Americans but was quickly immobilized. Sampson then went on to lead a blockade of and an attack on San Juan Harbor in Puerto Rico.

After the end of the war, Sampson remained in command of the navy's Atlantic fleet. In 1899, he was promoted to rear admiral and placed in charge of the Boston navy yard. He died in 1902.

Pascual Cervera y Topete was born in Medina-Sidonia, Cádiz, Spain, in 1839. He studied at the Naval Academy of San Fernando and began a career in the Spanish navy. By 1898, he was a navy admiral.

At the outset of the Spanish-American War, Cervera and his fleet were ordered to sail from Spain to Cuba to assist the Spanish military that already was in place. He felt the fleet was undersupplied and wished to postpone the assignment to regroup his forces but was directed to leave immediately for Cuba. Most of the Spanish army was clustered in Havana. In order to cover the lesser-defended part of the island, Cervera headed to Santiago de Cuba on the southern coast. His fleet landed there on May 19.

Admiral Pascual Cervera y Topote tried to break through the U.S. naval blockade of Cuba but had all his ships destroyed.

Throughout June, Cervera's forces were blockaded and rendered immobile by the U.S. naval fleet. It was a major turning point in the war. The blockade allowed the U.S. Army to link up with the U.S. Navy and attack Santiago de Cuba. U.S. president William McKinley was so certain of victory that, through contacts in Austria and Britain, he revealed to Spain his plan to occupy the Spanish colonies of Puerto Rico and Guam and take control of one port city in the Philippines.

Cervera, frustrated by being boxed in, attempted to break through the blockade at the beginning of July. Despite a heroic effort, all his ships were quickly wiped out. He was captured and became a prisoner of war. The incarceration of such a high-ranking Spanish naval officer was a major triumph for the United States.

Cervera was released from custody in September and departed for Spain. There, he was put on trial for the loss of his command at Santiago de Cuba, but his underlings offered evidence that the defeat was not his responsibility.

Cervera then held a number of positions within the Spanish government until he retired. He died in 1909.

Cervera was ordered to sail from Spain to Cuba despite his worries that the fleet was undersupplied.

THEODORE ROOSEVELT

Theodore Roosevelt was born in New York City in 1858. After he graduated from Harvard and operated a ranch in the Dakota Territory, he entered politics and was elected to the New York State Assembly. After an unsuccessful campaign for election as New York City mayor, he became commissioner first of the U.S. Civil Service and then the New York City Police Department.

Roosevelt's involvement in the Spanish-American War as both policy maker and soldier was essential to the quick U.S. victory. In 1897–1898, he was an assistant secretary of the U.S. Navy, and he believed that a war between America and Spain was inevitable. For this reason, he promoted the expansion of navy resources and renovation of its battleships. His emphasis on military preparedness proved crucial to commodore George Dewey's quick triumph over the Spanish fleet in Manila Bay at the onset of the war.

Roosevelt was not content to remain a Washington, D.C., policy maker. He resigned his navy post and, with Colonel Leonard Wood, a U.S. Army doctor, organized the Rough Riders, more formally known as the First United States Volunteer Cavalry. Roosevelt was second in command of the unit, which consisted of nonmilitary personnel: ranchers, Indians, cowboys, and sportsmen who were eager to find adventure while fighting on behalf of the United States.

The Rough Riders were attached to the U.S. Fifth Army Corps. They landed on Cuba's southern coast in June 1898 and made their way on horseback toward the city of Santiago de Cuba. On July 1, they were entrusted with assisting in the taking of San Juan Heights, which consisted of San Juan Hill and Kettle Hill, the high ground overlooking the city. Roosevelt led the Rough Riders into battle and urged them to victory despite mounting casualties.

The U.S. success at Santiago de Cuba was the final important military encounter of the Spanish-American War's Cuban campaign. For his heroics, Roosevelt was acclaimed a war hero. Success came at a high cost, however, as many of the Rough Riders became ill or were wounded or killed in action.

Theodore Roosevelt's stress on military preparation helped assure American victory in the war.

After the war, Roosevelt was elected governor of New York and vice president in William McKinley's successful 1900 reelection bid. When McKinley was assassinated the following year, Roosevelt became the twenty-sixth U.S. president and was returned to office in 1904. He left the White House four years later but remained active in national politics. He died in 1919.

Roosevelt leads the Rough Riders at the Battle of San Juan Hill in Cuba. He became a war hero and later served as president of the United States.

NELSON A. MILES

DIRECTED MILITARY OPERATIONS IN CUBA AND PUERTO RICO

Nelson Appleton Miles was born near Westminster, Massachusetts, in 1839. He volunteered to fight for the Union in the Civil War, emerged a major general, and won the Congressional Medal of Honor. As a cavalry commander, he conducted military offensives against Indian tribes in the American West during the 1870s and 1880s.

In 1895, Miles was named commanding general and commander in chief of the U.S. Army. In this capacity, he played a major part on several fronts during and directly after the Spanish-American War. Despite his title, Miles's role at the outset of the war was primarily administrative, as he was charged with overseeing the organization and training of the American military. However, he was destined to take an active role in the fighting.

U.S. Army commander Nelson A. Miles's troops prepare to leave for the Spanish-American War.

Miles wished to give special attention to the conquest of Puerto Rico and, after the Spanish surrendered Santiago de Cuba, he personally led U.S. troops in an assault on the island. On July 25, 1898, he and his forces arrived in Guánica, a small town on Puerto Rico's southern coast. After they took Ponce, another coastal settlement, he headed northward to San Juan and sporadically battled Spanish troops. Before his troops could occupy San Juan, notification of a peace settlement arrived and the fighting ceased.

In addition to leading the force that took Puerto Rico from the Spanish, Miles became the first head of the island's postwar military government. He was charged with overseeing the army of occupation and the island's municipal affairs.

Miles was promoted to lieutenant general in 1900. Two years later, he traveled to the Philippines, where nationalists were battling the American occupation forces. He spoke with U.S. troops and Filipino administrators, scrutinized the situation, and issued a controversial report that highlighted American abuses against the Filipinos.

After he retired from the military in 1903, Miles spent his remaining years writing books and serving on various government and nongovernment committees. He died in 1925.

Miles led his troops in attacks on several coastal settlements. The war ended before he could take San Juan.

Cuban revolutionary Máximo Gómez y Báez received help from the Americans in his fight for Cuba's freedom.

MÁXIMO GÓMEZ Y BÁEZ

BATTLED SPAIN DURING THE FIGHT FOR CUBAN INDEPENDENCE

Máximo Gómez y Báez was born in Baní, Dominican Republic, in 1836. His studies at a religious school were disrupted upon a Haitian invasion of his homeland in the mid-1850s. He fought with his countrymen against the Haitians, became a captain in the Dominican army reserve, and in 1865 relocated to Santiago de Cuba.

Although not a native Cuban, Gómez favored Cuban independence and played a significant role in the island's liberation from Spain. As early as the late 1860s, he was active in the struggle for freedom. First, he commanded Cuban nationalists during the unsuccessful Ten Years War against Spain. Then, he backed the Guerra Chiquita, or Little War, another failed effort to win Cuba's freedom.

While in New York in 1884, Gómez befriended José Martí, the famed Cuban poet and nationalist. Eight years later, at the request of Martí, Gómez took charge of the military tactics of the Cuban revolution that culminated in the Spanish-American War. After three years of planning, the revolution began in February 1895.

Gómez devised and instigated a series of hit-and-run attacks on the Spanish occupation force. He refused to negotiate with the Spanish; complete independence was the objective. With the U.S. declaration of war against Spain in April 1898, he collaborated with the Americans, who provided him with

Gómez toured Cuba after Spain and the United States signed the Treaty of Paris, ending the Spanish-American War.

armaments. At the August cease-fire, he took sanctuary on a sugar plantation in Las Villas Province to await the Spanish withdrawal. The war officially ended on December 10, upon the signing of the Treaty of Paris. At that point, Gómez toured the island. Amid much jubilation, he arrived in Havana on February 24, 1899.

Gómez emerged from the war a hero of Cuba and continued to look out for the rights of the Cuban people. He feared that the Americans wished to unduly influence Cuba's internal affairs, and he clashed with the new Cuban Assembly when he announced his opposition to a proposed loan from the United States.

In his later years, Gómez remained involved in Cuban politics. He died in 1905.

Clarissa Harlowe Barton was born in North Oxford, Massachusetts, in 1821. At age seventeen, she began working as a teacher in Worcester County, Massachusetts, and eventually opened her own school in Bordentown, New Jersey.

When the local school board denied her application to supervise the school and instead hired a man, she moved to Washington, D.C. There, she became a U.S. Patent Office clerk. During the Civil War (1861–1865), Barton volunteered to deliver medical supplies to the front lines and work as a nursing administrator. In 1881, she founded the American Red Cross and became its first president.

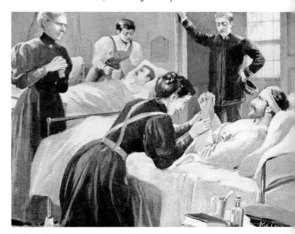

Clara Barton supervises nurses in a Havana hospital as they tend to men injured in the sinking of the USS Maine.

Before the Spanish-American War, the American Red Cross had assisted victims of floods, famines, earthquakes, and yellow fever epidemics. It saw its first battlefield service in Cuba, before and during the war. Barton and several staff members arrived in Cuba on February 9, 1898, a week before the sinking of the USS *Maine*. As tensions worsened, she and her workers transported medical supplies to hospitals, handed out clothing, and opened soup kitchens and orphanages. Their efforts intensified when war was declared. They nursed those injured in battle and faced dangerous epidemics of yellow fever, malaria, dysentery, and typhoid.

Despite the tropical climate and her advanced age—she was in her late seventies—Barton personally spearheaded efforts to nurse wounded soldiers, rebels, civilians, and prisoners of war. She reportedly toiled for sixteen hours each day to tend to the sick and wounded. She journeyed in wagons pulled by mules to bring supplies to soldiers and civilians.

Barton headed the American Red Cross through 1904, when a combination of her age and a series of disagreements over the running of the organization forced her into retirement. She moved to her home in Glen Echo, Maryland, and died in 1912.

Barton was well into her seventies when she arrived in Cuba with medical supplies and workers.

⊙ CHRONOLOGY

January 5, 1892	El Partido Revolucionario Cubano (Cuban Revolutionary Party) is established by José Martí and other Cuban nationalists.
July 3, 1892	José Rizal establishes the Liga Filipina (Philippine League) to promote Filipino independence from Spain.
March 4, 1893	Grover Cleveland begins his second term as U.S. president.
February 24, 1895	The revolution in Cuba begins.
May 19, 1895	Martí dies while fighting the Spanish in Dos Rios.
June 12, 1895	Cleveland signs a proclamation declaring that the United States will maintain its neutrality in any war between Spain and its colonies.
February 10, 1896	Valeriano Weyler is appointed governor of Cuba.
December 30, 1896	Rizal is executed by a Spanish firing squad.
March 4, 1897	William McKinley replaces Cleveland as U.S. president.
November 1897	Spanish president Práxedes Mateo Sagasta agrees to allow Cuba and Puerto Rico self-ruling governments; the Cuban nationalists reject the offer.
February 9, 1898	The *New York Journal* publishes the de Lóme letter; Clara Barton arrives in Cuba to tend to wounded Cuban rebels and citizens.
February 15, 1898	An explosion aboard the USS *Maine* kills 266 U.S. sailors.
March 9, 1898	The U.S. Congress authorizes the spending of $50 million to strengthen the U.S. military.
March 29, 1898	A U.S. Navy court of inquiry determines that the USS *Maine* was destroyed by a mine.

April 20, 1898	The U.S. Congress declares war on Spain.
April 21, 1898	McKinley directs that the U.S. Navy put into effect a blockade of Cuba.
May 1, 1898	Commodore George Dewey leads the U.S. Navy into Manila Bay.
May 19, 1898	The Spanish fleet arrives in Santiago de Cuba.
June 1, 1989	The U.S. Navy corners the Spanish fleet in the harbor of Santiago de Cuba.
June 15, 1898	The Anti-Imperialist League is formed to oppose the U.S. annexation of the Philippines.
June 22, 1898	Theodore Roosevelt's Rough Riders land in Cuba.
July 1, 1898	U.S. forces battle the Spanish at Santiago de Cuba.
July 17, 1898	The Spanish surrender Santiago de Cuba.
July 25, 1898	The U.S. military arrives in Guánica, Puerto Rico, to begin an offensive against the Spanish.
August 12, 1898	All fighting in the Spanish-American war ceases.
October 1, 1898	Representatives of the United States and Spain meet in Paris and begin negotiating the treaty that officially will end the war.
December 10, 1898	The Treaty of Paris is signed; Cuba becomes a free nation; Puerto Rico, Guam, and the Philippines are annexed by the United States.
February 6, 1899	The U.S. Senate ratifies the Treaty of Paris.
1898–1902	Emilio Aguinaldo y Famy and other Filipino nationalists unsuccessfully battle the Americans for control of their homeland.

FOR FURTHER INFORMATION

BOOKS

Edward F. Dolan, *The Spanish-American War.* Brookfield, CT: Millbrook, 2001.

Michael Golay, *Spanish-American War.* New York: Facts On File, 1995.

Tom McGowen, *The Spanish-American War and Teddy Roosevelt in American History.* Berkeley Heights, NJ: Enslow, 2003.

Robert Somerlott, *The Spanish-American War: "Remember the Maine!"* Berkeley Heights, NJ: Enslow, 2002.

David F. Trask, *The War With Spain in 1898.* New York: Macmillan, 1981. Reprint, Lincoln: University of Nebraska Press, 1996.

John F. Wukovits, *The Spanish-American War.* San Diego: Lucent, 2002.

WEB SITES

Crucible of Empire: The Spanish-American War
www.pbs.org/crucible
An overview of the war, presented by the Public Broadcasting Service (PBS).

A War in Perspective, 1898–1898
www.nypl.org/research/chss/epo/spanexhib
An overview of the Spanish-American War, presented by the New York Public Library.

The World of 1898: The Spanish-American War
www.loc.gov/rr/hispanic/1898
An overview of the war, presented by the Library of Congress.

PICTURE CREDITS

Cover:
background, upper left, lower right, © CORBIS
Upper right, lower left, © Bettmann/CORBIS
Lower middle, Hulton Archive by Getty images

© Bettmann/CORBIS, 11, 16, 27, 35, 42, 43

© CORBIS, 12, 15, 23, 25, 28-29, 36-37, 39

© Hulton-Deutsch Collection/CORBIS, 10

© Oscar White/CORBIS, 8

Hulton Archives by Getty Images, 9, 31, 32, 38

Library of Congress, 20, 40, 41

National Archives, 18-19, 22, 24, 33

National Portrait Gallery, 30

New York Historical Society, 14

ABOUT THE AUTHOR

Audrey Kupferberg is a writer and film historian who teaches at the University of Albany (SUNY). She lives in Amsterdam, New York, with her husband Rob Edelman, with whom she has authored books on movie and television personalities. She enjoys playing racquetball and golf.

INDEX